LEGENDS OF WARFARE

AVIATION

F8F Bearcat

Grumman's Late-War Dogfighter

DAVID DOYLE

SCHIFFER MILITARY

4880 Lower Valley Road ∎ Atglen, PA 19310

Designed by Christopher Bower
Cover design by Justin Watkinson
Front cover image by Rich Kalosa
Type set in Impact/Minion Pro/Univers LT Std

ISBN: 978-0-7643-6701-4
Printed in India

Published by Schiffer Publishing, Ltd.
4880 Lower Valley Road
Atglen, PA 19310
Phone: (610) 593-1777; Fax: (610) 593-2002
Email: Info@schifferbooks.com
Web: www.schifferbooks.com

For our complete selection of fine books on this and related subjects, please visit our website at www.schifferbooks.com. You may also write for a free catalog.

Schiffer Publishing's titles are available at special discounts for bulk purchases for sales promotions or premiums. Special editions, including personalized covers, corporate imprints, and excerpts, can be created in large quantities for special needs. For more information, contact the publisher.

We are always looking for people to write books on new and related subjects. If you have an idea for a book, please contact us at proposals@schifferbooks.com.

Acknowledgments

This book would have been impossible to create without the help of a number of friends, including Tom Kailbourn, Rich Kolasa, Scott Taylor, Stan Piet, Brian Lockett, the late Leo Polaski, Roger Davis, the staff and volunteers at the National Museum of Naval Aviation, Robert Hanshew at the Naval History and Heritage Command, and Brett Stolle at the National Museum of the United States Air Force. Of course my best friend, my wife, Denise, was continuously supportive during the creation of this book.

Contents

Introduction

In the summer of 1943, Grumman's plant in Bethpage, Long Island, was turning out the F6F Hellcat at a prodigious rate, but work on an improved Navy fighter was about to begin. What was desired was a lighter, more compact aircraft that could outclimb and outfly Japanese fighters yet operate from small escort carriers. The characteristics of this new aircraft, Grumman model number G58, were outlined by Leroy Grumman in a memo to chief engineer William Schwendler on July 28, 1943.

Numerous stories circulate indicating that the design inspiration of the aircraft that would become the Bearcat (model G58) was derived from the evaluation in England of a captured German Focke-Wulf Fw 190A by Leroy Grumman and Robert Hall in September 1943. However, as we have seen, Leroy Grumman had drafted the Bearcat's specifications more than a month prior to the trip across the Atlantic and evaluation of the German aircraft. So, while examination of the Fw 190 may have led to some refinement, the design originated with Leroy Grumman, not Focke-Wulf's Kurt Tank.

The Navy assigned the new aircraft the designation of XF8F-1, and two prototypes were ordered in November 1943. The first prototype of the new plane, dubbed "Bearcat," did not fly until August 21, 1944, only nine months after the contract was signed.

At the controls that day was Grumman chief engineer and test pilot Robert Hall.

In the interim, impressed with the design presented by Grumman, the Navy had ordered a further twenty-three evaluation aircraft. Flight-testing of the XF8F indicated an impressive 4,800-feet-per-minute climb rate, clearly satisfying the high-rate-of-climb goal that had been urged by ace John Smith "Jimmy" Thach during a meeting with Leroy Grumman back on June 23, 1942.

The aircraft was powered by the same Pratt & Whitney R-2800 used in the F6F Hellcat, and accordingly the improved performance was the result of a strenuous effort to reduce the weight of the aircraft. In large part this was done using a 5-foot-shorter airframe and a reduction in armament and fuel capacity.

The first of the prototypes, Bureau Number (BuNo) 90460, was lost in a fatal crash into Chesapeake Bay while flying out of Naval Air Station Patuxent River on March 18, 1945, with Lt. David L. Mandt at the controls.

In the early days of the US involvement in World War II, US Navy fighters were typified by Grumman products such as this F4F Wildcat—notably rugged, but not notably fast or maneuverable. *National Archives*

The lessons learned early in the war were taken to heart, and a new Grumman fighter, the F6F Hellcat, was created. Although the Hellcat racked an impressive score, being credited with destroying over five thousand enemy aircraft, the threat of kamikaze attacks was one of the reasons the Navy sought an aircraft with a faster time-to-climb rate. That aircraft would be the F8F. *National Archives*

Grumman produced two prototypes of the Bearcat, designated XF8F-1 and assigned US Navy Bureau Numbers (BuNo) 90460 and 90461. The first prototype, BuNo 90460, shown here, first flew on August 31, 1944, with Grumman test pilot Bob Hall at the controls. The Navy tested this plane for catapult takeoffs and arrested landings on carriers at Naval Air Station Mustin Field, Philadelphia, in November 1944. Following full-scale wind-tunnel tests at NACA Ames, in Sunnyvale, California, the first prototype was undergoing weapons testing at NATC Patuxent River, Maryland, when it was destroyed in a crash in March 1945. *National Museum of Naval Aviation*

In February 1945, a partially finished Bearcat is suspended above the Grumman factory floor, about to be subjected to a three-point drop test. It was important to verify before the aircraft was delivered to the Navy that it could withstand hard landings. *Grumman Memorial Park via Leo Polaski*

A Bearcat undergoes drop tests to determine the strength of the landing gear during hard landings on January 29, 1945. A large weight has been fastened to the engine mount to simulate the weight of the Pratt & Whitney R-2800 engine once installed. *Grumman Memorial Park via Leo Polaski*

The first Bearcat prototype, XF8F-1, BuNo 90460, is poised on a hardstand with a test pilot in the cockpit on September 21, 1944, during the first month of testing of this aircraft. This plane achieved a maximum speed of 434 miles per hour during tests. *Grumman Memorial Park via Leo Polaski*

On the first prototype, the wing-fold mechanism is visible. After the plane's first flight, test pilot Bob Hall advised that it was necessary to increase the span of the horizontal stabilizers by 2 feet to improve stability; Grumman immediately made the change. *Grumman Memorial Park via Leo Polaski*

Viewed from aft, the first prototype, BuNo 90460, displays its wings in the folded position. The wing-fold design was simpler than that of the Grumman F4F Wildcat or F6F Hellcat's rearward-folding wings. The Bearcat's wings were folded manually, using a detachable wing-folding bar. *Grumman Memorial Park via Leo Polaski*

In the leading edge of each wing, near the fuselage, is a split air intake. The outboard part of the intake is for induction air, and the inboard part of the intake is for the oil cooler. Both of the prototype XF8F-1s had the Aeroproducts A642-G1 constant-speed propeller. *Grumman Memorial Park via Leo Polaski*

This photo of XF8F-1, BuNo 90460, was taken on the same occasion as the preceding photograph, only showing the wings fully extended. There appear to be markings on two of the propeller blades, possibly sprayed paint, perhaps for testing or calibrating purposes, *Naval History and Heritage Command*

The first prototype, XF8F-1, BuNo 90460, makes a test flight. Attempts by Grumman to engineer a cleanly breaking joint 40 inches from the wingtips, so the plane would remain controllable should an outer wing break during high-g flight, were ultimately abandoned. *Grumman Memorial Park via Leo Polaski*

XF8F-1, BuNo 90460, seen in the preceding photos, is viewed here during a monthlong program of testing at NACA Ames, Sunnyvale, California, in February 1945. A fillet has here been added to the lower front of the vertical stabilizer. *NASA Langley Research Center*

An early-model Bearcat cockpit, most likely in XF8F-1, BuNo 90460, is depicted in a February 26, 1945, photo. At the bottom is the pilot's seat pan, immediately forward of which is the control stick, with a prominent accordion-action boot at the bottom. The instrument panel is fairly compact, as befitted the small size of the aircraft. At the top of the instrument panel is a Mk. 8 reflecting-type gunsight. On each side of the cockpit is a console. The throttle quadrant is above the left console. Above the right console is a hand crank for operating the sliding canopy. *Grumman Memorial Park via Leo Polaski*

CHAPTER 1
F8F-1

F8F-1, BuNo 90438, rests on the flight deck of the escort carrier USS *Charger* (CVE-30) in February 1945. The occasion was the first carrier-sustainability trials of the Bearcat. The pilot of the plane was Lt. Cmdr. Robert Martin Elder (1918–2008), who had distinguished himself as a combat pilot in World War II. In spite of poor weather conditions, Elder completed fifteen arrested landings on the carrier. For his combat exploits, Elder was awarded the Navy Cross and the Distinguished Flying Cross. He later went on to prominence in naval aircraft-testing programs. After retiring from the Navy in 1963, he was instrumental in Northrop's testing programs. *National Museum of Naval Aviation*

The twenty-three evaluation aircraft ordered in October 1943 were built to production standards, and Grumman records list the aircraft as F8F-1 models. Subsequent orders increased the number of F8F aircraft on order with Grumman by two thousand units.

In addition, in February 1945, just as Grumman was beginning to make the first service deliveries of the F8F, the Navy ordered an additional 1,876 Bearcats from the Eastern Aircraft Division of General Motors. Eastern was already building duplicates of the Grumman Wildcat and Avenger. The GM-built Bearcats were to be designated the F3M-1.

The Navy ordered that the thirty-seventh production F8F-1, BuNo 94765, be delivered to the Eastern Aircraft plant in Linden, New Jersey, to serve as a sample aircraft. This was done on June 10, 1945.

As mentioned, Grumman began service deliveries in February 1945, and the first F8F-equipped fleet unit, Fighter Squadron 19 (VF-19), became operational in May 1945.

As a weight-saving measure, the F8F-1 was armed with four .50-caliber machine guns (rather than the six heavy machine guns carried by the Hellcats and Corsairs). This reduction in armament was not met with enthusiasm by the pilots, and given the growing number of kamikaze attacks, by August 1945, steps were undertaken to upgrade the armament to four 20 mm cannon.

Nighttime aerial combat moved to the forefront in Europe even before the US became involved in the war. As tactics were honed, the US Navy formed twenty-five night-fighting squadrons between April 1943 and June 1945, while the US Marines formed an additional seven between November 1942 and May 1944.

During this time, the F6F Hellcat formed the backbone of carrier-borne night-fighter squadrons. Naturally, as the F8F began to supplant the Hellcat, attention was turned to creating a night-fighter variant of the Bearcat as well. During the summer of 1945,

test installations of radar equipment were made with F8F serial numbers 94812 and 94819. While the Hellcat-based night fighters used the AN/APS-6 radar, the diminutive Bearcat used the newly developed Sperry AN/APS-19 radar set. Despite being smaller than its predecessor, the limited space between the guns and wing fold of the Bearcat prevented the system from being embedded in the leading edge of the wing, which was the radar-mounting method used on F6F night fighters. Instead, the AN/APS-19 radar had to be hung from the starboard wing bomb rack.

Following those tests, twelve F8F-1 aircraft were modified by Grumman while still on the assembly line into F8F-1N night fighters. Like their experimental predecessors, the F8F-1N carried its radar pod on the starboard bomb rack. Ultimately, the Navy decided that other aircraft were better suited for the role of night fighter, and the operational use of the F8F-1N was limited to operational testing by VCN-1 and VCN-2.

The dropping of the atomic bombs, however, brought the war to an end before the F8F could be used for the duty it had come to be expected to perform—intercepting kamikazes. Indeed, the F8F saw no combat at all during World War II.

The end of the war brought with it significant cancellations of F8F orders, as it did with much material. Grumman's order was reduced to 770 aircraft, and the Eastern Aircraft order was canceled completely. As a result, no F3M-1s were ever built.

However, an additional 126 F8F-1s were ordered and built with cannon armament. These aircraft, F8F-1B, are referred to in some texts as F8F-1C, reflecting an early, briefly used designation for the type. The last of these aircraft were delivered in August 1947. The last of the 664 baseline F8F-1 aircraft was delivered in November 1947.

The F8F-1 was the first production model of the Bearcat. Here, a pilot flies a training mission in F8F-1, BuNo 95443, serving with Carrier Aircraft Service Unit 1 (CASU-1), based at NAS Ford Island, Pearl Harbor, on July 27, 1945. This unit was tasked with preparing pilots for flying aircraft, in this case the F8F-1, in carrier operations. The letter "I" on the fuselage refers to the unit, while 40 is the individual aircraft number. Underneath the fuselage is a 150-gallon drop tank. *National Museum of the United States Air Force*

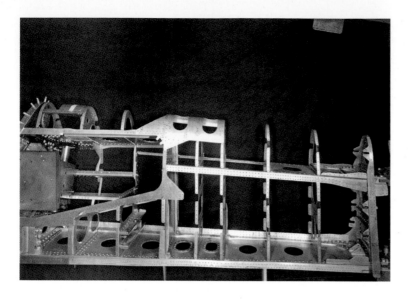

A July 19, 1944, photo shows part of the inboard port wing frame of a Bearcat under construction. To the left is the outboard part of the opening for the main landing-gear bay. At the top center are two oval ports for the wing-mounted machine guns. *Grumman Memorial Park via Leo Polaski*

The same partial inboard wing frame seen in the preceding photograph is viewed in its construction jig from the wing's upper side. At the bottom is the main spar; to the left are several wing ribs, perforated with lightening holes of various shapes. *Grumman Memorial Park via Leo Polaski*

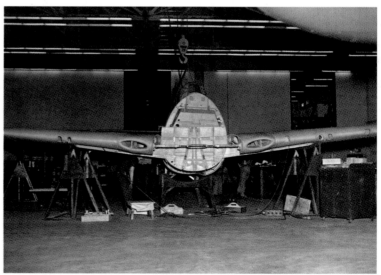

The interior of the rear section of a Bearcat fuselage is viewed facing forward in this 1944 photograph. Several pieces of radio equipment are mounted aft of the rear bulkhead of the cockpit, and in the D-shaped recess to the right is an oxygen bottle. *Grumman Memorial Park via Leo Polaski*

An F8F-1 airframe on stands appears to be under construction at Grumman Aircraft on January 13, 1945. The wings, including the leading edges and the air intakes, are clad with aluminum alloy skin, but the engine and cowl have not yet been installed. *Grumman Memorial Park via Leo Polaski*

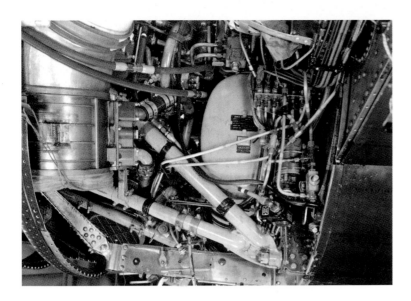

The lower part of the port side of the engine accessory apartment of a Bearcat is displayed in an October 1944 photo. To the left is the left oil cooler. The V-shaped tubular assembly is part of the engine mount; above it is the hydraulic distribution unit. *Grumman Memorial Park via Leo Polaski*

The panels have been removed from the left console in the cockpit of an early Bearcat in this July 5, 1945, photo, exposing various lines. To the left is the aft bulkhead of the cockpit, while to the upper right is the throttle quadrant and fuel mixture control. *Grumman Memorial Park via Leo Polaski*

Flown by Lt. A. M. "Mike" Granat, this F8F-1 (BuNo 95081) was assigned to VF-3 "Felix the Cat" in early 1946.

Grumman workers fabricated a number of display boards on rollers to exhibit the layout of various systems of the F8F-1. This display shows the electrical systems. At the lower center is the right cockpit console, and above it is the instrument panel. *Grumman Memorial Park via Leo Polaski*

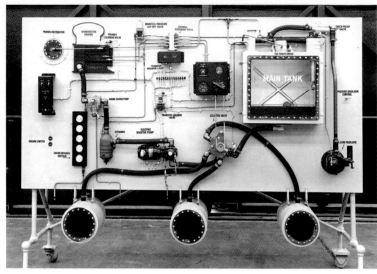

The layout of the fuel system is displayed here. To the top right is a representation of the main fuel tank, which was located below the cockpit. The three cylindrical objects below the board represent drop tanks: two under the wings and one under the fuselage. *Grumman Memorial Park via Leo Polaski*

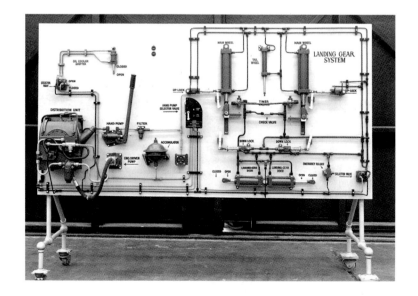

In a display of the landing-gear system, to the lower left is the hydraulic distribution unit, to the right of which is the hand pump for emergency operation of the landing gear. Operating cylinders for the main and tail landing gear and gear doors are to the right. *Grumman Memorial Park via Leo Polaski*

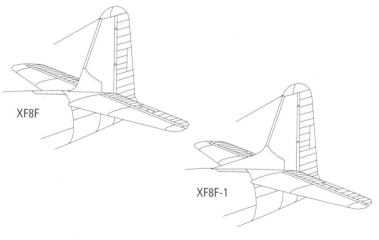

While the Bearcat's bubble canopy provided excellent visibility, critical for fighter pilots, it inherently did away with the "razorback" that characterized the F4F and F6F. The lack of this razorback adversely affected aircraft handling during spins. Accordingly, a dorsal fin was added to the production models.

A Grumman F8F-1 Bearcat rests on a tarmac on March 20, 1945. The BuNo on the vertical stabilizer is indistinct but appears to be 90441. If so, that would make this the fifth production F8F-1. The nearly straight wing-fold joints are visible. The F8F-1 was similar to the XF8F-1, with several exceptions: The production aircraft had the Pratt & Whitney R-2800-34W radial engine, whereas the first prototype had the P&W R-2800-10B and the second prototype was equipped with the R-2800-22W engine. The F8F-1 also had a 183-gallon fuel capacity, 21 gallons more than the XF8F-1. Provisions were also included for carrying auxiliary fuel and munitions under the centerline and under the wings. *Grumman Memorial Park via Leo Polaski*

An F8F-1 is undergoing stress tests to gauge the elasticity of the airframe on July 20, 1945. Instead of the two .50-caliber machine guns that are usually found in each wing of the F8F-1, two 20 mm cannons have been installed in the same positions, perhaps experimentally. *Grumman Memorial Park via Leo Polaski*

The F8F-1 Bearcat was slightly underarmed with its four wing-mounted .50-caliber machine guns (its predecessor, the F6F, had six .50s). To give the plane more punch, Douglas Aircraft developed wing-mounted twin .50-caliber machine gun pods. *Grumman Memorial Park via Leo Polaski*

A ground crewman stands on the left wing of an F8F-1 Bearcat with its engine being warmed up, at an unidentified base in the Pacific around mid-1945. Wooden chocks are snugged around the tires. A fire extinguisher is next to the left main landing gear; this equipment was always kept nearby when an aircraft was being started. Aircraft to the rear are, *left to right*, an F4U Corsair, a TBF/TBM Avenger, and an SB2C Helldiver.

A Lt. Schertz rolled over this F8F-1, BuNo 94841, during an emergency landing at Grumman's airfield at Bethpage, Long Island, on August 1, 1945. Schertz had been attempting to deliver the plane to NAS Floyd Bennett Field in Brooklyn, New York. *Grumman Memorial Park via Leo Polaski*

This Bearcat, F8F-1, BuNo 94819, converted to an XF8F-1N prototype night fighter, has been righted on its landing gear after test pilot Pat Gallo belly-landed the plane in August 1945 at Grumman's Bethpage airfield. On the ground is the AN/APS-19 radar pod. *Grumman Memorial Park via Leo Polaski*

Even after the Bearcat went into production, Grumman continued experimenting with ways to enable clean breaks in the outer wing if the wing failed during high-g maneuvers. F8F-1, BuNo 95802, is shown after one such experiment in February 1946. *Grumman Memorial Park via Leo Polaski*

Cockpit canopy open, an F8F-1 assigned to VF-18 takes off from the flight deck of USS *Ranger* (CV-4) as ship's personnel look on from the island of the carrier. The squadron was embarked on the ship en route from San Diego to New Orleans via the Panama Canal. *National Museum of Naval Aviation*

Deck crewmen on USS *Ranger* shove an F8F-1 of VF-18 into place during the San Diego–New Orleans redeployment in 1945. The letter "K" on the fuselage side was the identification code assigned to the carrier USS *Langley* (CVL-27) in July 1945. *National Museum of Naval Aviation*

Lt. Cmdr. D. C. "Whiff" Caldwell flies his F8F-1 over the mountains near San Francisco, California, on June 2, 1947. He was the commander of VF-20A, assigned to USS *Boxer* (CV-21). Caldwell's campaign ribbons are painted on the cowl. *National Museum of Naval Aviation*

An F8F-1 assigned to the commanding officer of VF-19 nears the forward end of the flight deck of USS *Antietam* (CV-36) during a takeoff on April 11, 1946. The squadron was assigned to that aircraft carrier from April to late August 1946. *National Museum of Naval Aviation*

Members of the catapult crew are at work as an F8F is being launched from the Essex-class aircraft carrier USS *Randolph* (CV-15) on June 10, 1947. The aircraft is marked with side number 125 on the fuselage and the right wing, and the letter "K" on the tail and the right wing indicates Carrier Air Group 3.

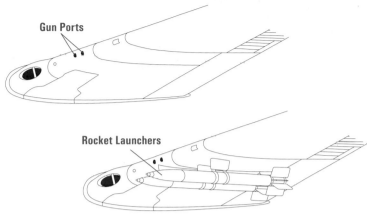

Gun Ports

Rocket Launchers

Resting at Naval Air Station North Island, Coronado, this F8F-1 Bearcat, serial number 95343, was assigned to VF-11A, the famed "Sun Downers," in 1947. The unit and its Bearcats would be deployed aboard USS *Valley Forge* that year and embark upon a world cruise that would last until June 1948. *San Diego Air and Space Museum*

Late-production F8F-1 aircraft were equipped with two Mk. 9 rocket launchers beneath each wing. These launchers could accommodate the 5-inch High Velocity Aircraft Rocket (HVAR) fin-stabilized rockets. Each of these rockets weighed approximately 134 pounds.

Off the coast of Southern California in July 1948, an F8F-1 Bearcat assigned to VF-16A prepares to move forward on the flight deck of USS *Tarawa* (CV-40). The name of the pilot, Lt. j.g. Guyer, is stenciled in white above the number 211 on the fuselage. The aircraft number, Carrier Air Group (CVAG) 15's identification code letter A, and the top of the vertical stabilizer and rudder were painted Insignia White, signifying the second squadron in the group. The thin, diagonal white line on the fuselage helped indicate the locations of a recessed step at the bottom and a recessed handhold at the top. Underneath the canopy, behind the pilot's armor, the rollover crash-protection arch is visible. *National Museum of Naval Aviation*

In a companion piece to the preceding photograph, F8F-1s of CVAG-15 warm their engines on USS *Tarawa* in July 1948. Deck crewmen stand by to remove the chocks from the wheels of the planes. The nearest aircraft has horizontal red and yellow stripes painted on its tail and on its rudder trim tab. Its propeller hub and rudder / vertical stabilizer tip are red, signifying the first squadron in the air group, VF-15A, while those on the next Bearcat in line are white, for VF-16A. The aircraft number and group code are repeated on the starboard wing tops and under the port wings. The month this photo was taken, VF-15A and VF-16A were redesignated VF-151 and VF-152, respectively. *National Museum of Naval Aviation*

Three of CVAG-15's F8F-1s (*left to right*: numbers 205, 105, and 211) are parked on the flight deck of USS *Tarawa* in July 1948. Each has a centerline drop tank mounted. In the background with wings folded are several Douglas Skyraider attack aircraft. *National Museum of Naval Aviation*

A Grumman F8F-1, BuNo 94926, is spotted on a tarmac at Naval Air Test Center (NATC) Patuxent River, Maryland, on July 9, 1948. White stencils are visible on the airframe, including "ENCLOSURE RELEASE" below the windscreen, and "TIRE PRESSURE / NORMAL 115 LBS" on the bottom of the main landing-gear fairing.

Cmdr. William F. "Bush" Bringle, commander of Air Group 1, turns to face the photographer as he flies his F8F-1, BuNo 95131, out of Moffatt Field, California, on October 4, 1948. A Navy Cross recipient, Bringle went on to become a four-star admiral. *National Museum of Naval Aviation*

The pilot of an F8F-1 of VF-31 "Tomcatters," assigned to USS *Kearsarge* (CV-33) struggles to get free of the cockpit after crashing into the ocean during 1949. The vertical tail has become crumpled during the crash. A pilot who got "feet wet" close to a carrier group had excellent odds of being rescued quickly, either by a shipborne helicopter or by an escort craft. *National Museum of Naval Aviation*

Near sunset on November 4, 1948, an F8F Bearcat fighter is making a landing approach to the Essex-class carrier USS *Tarawa* (CV-40) during a cruise in the western Pacific. To the starboard side of the aft part of the flight deck is the canvas windscreen for the landing-signal officer.

Because the F8F-1 was a "hot" plane to handle and pilots often lacked experience, training accidents were common with Bearcats. The following series of photos documents the March 1948 crash of F8F-1, BuNo 95398, on USS *Valley Forge* (CV-45). *National Museum of Naval Aviation*

The Bearcat, piloted by Ens. Eugene Bezore of VF-11A, has a nose-high attitude as it approaches the deck. Despite the proximity of the tailhook to the deck, it will fail to catch an arrestor wire, and it will be up to the barricade to stop the plane. *National Museum of Naval Aviation*

At the instant the preceding photo was taken, another photographer on the port side of USS *Valley Forge*'s flight deck snapped this photo of Ens. Bezore's F8F-1 struggling to catch the arrestor wire. The wires of the barricade are visible to the front of the plane. *National Museum of Naval Aviation*

The wires of the barricade have arrested Ens. Bezore's Bearcat, and the plane is in the process of flipping over. Although the barricade presented a traumatic and violent means of stopping an aircraft, it could also prevent catastrophic damage to planes on the deck. *National Museum of Naval Aviation*

Deck crewmen on USS *Valley Forge* scramble to secure Ens. Bezore's F8F-1 after it has come to rest upside down on the flight deck. The propeller blades are badly bent, and the tailhook is still extended. On this day, the pilot's armor and attached rollover crash-protection arch did their job, since Bezore survived the crash. He went on to enjoy a long and distinguished career in the US Navy, flying F9F Panther fighters in the Korean War and serving as executive officer of VF-103 in the 1960s and later as air warfare officer of the Sixth Fleet Staff. *National Museum of Naval Aviation*

Using small, handheld signal paddles, a landing-signal officer (LSO) behind a windscreen on USS *Valley Forge* waves off an approaching F8F-1. Planes approaching at a speed or attitude unfeasible for landing were signaled to go around for another attempt. *National Museum of Naval Aviation*

The tailhook of this F8F-1 assigned to VF-15A has snagged an arrestor wire on USS *Tarawa* during July 1948. Additional arrestor wires were rigged across the flight deck, held in a slightly raised position, in case a plane failed to catch the first wire. *National Museum of Naval Aviation*

F8F-1 Bearcats of VF-15A and VF-16A prepare for takeoff aboard USS *Tarawa* (CV-40) in July 1948. The plane marked number 205 to the right and the two planes aft of it were assigned to VF-16A, as indicated by the white tops of the rudders and vertical stabilizers. The other two Bearcats had red rudders and fin tops, indicating VF-15A. Under a directive of May 1, 1948, propeller hubs and the top 7 inches of the vertical tail and rudder of aircraft belonging to the first squadron in an air group were to be Insignia Red, while those features on the aircraft of the second squadron were to be Insignia White. In the background are Douglas Skyraiders of VA-15A. *National Museum of Naval Aviation*

The prolific photographer who took so many images of F8F-1 Bearcats of VF-15A and VF-16A aboard USS *Tarawa* (CV-40) during her July 1948 cruise captured this shot of several of the planes from aft as they warmed their engines preparatory to a mission. *National Museum of Naval Aviation*

Number 205, the F8F-1 Bearcat assigned to Lieutenant Baumeister, prepares for takeoff on USS *Tarawa* in July 1948. Deck crewmen are poised ready to remove the wheel chocks, and the cowl flaps are open. Whip antennas are on the fuselage top and bottom. *National Museum of Naval Aviation*

A tractor is maneuvering an F8F-1 on the flight deck of USS *Philippine Sea* (CV-47) during a snowstorm during fleet maneuvers in the North Atlantic on November 13, 1948. A single rocket is mounted under each wing. In the background is a Sikorsky HO3S helicopter, to the rear of which is the forward twin 5-inch/38-caliber gun mount, with "BEWARE PROPELLERS" stenciled on the front.

On August 13, 1948, F8F-1, BuNo 95318, of VF-192 (formerly VF-20A) makes a catapult launch from USS *Princeton* (CV-37). The catapult bridle can be seen underneath the plane; this is attached to the catapult shuttle, which is propelled along a track in the deck. *National Museum of Naval Aviation*

As the aircraft carrier USS *Valley Forge* (CV-45) approaches the Sydney Harbour Bridge, numerous F8Fs and, in the foreground, two Grumman TBM Avengers are spotted on the flight deck. The occasion was a visit to Sydney, Australia, during a training and goodwill cruise to the western Pacific in early 1948. *Valley Forge* was serving as the flagship of RAdm. H. M. Martin, commander of Task Force 38.

F8F-1, BuNo 95259, assigned to Cmdr. W. R. Barlow, commanding officer of VF- 19A, is poised on a tarmac at NAS Oakland, California, around early 1948. Mounted on the underwing pylon is a bomblet dispenser, a device used in bombing practice. *National Museum of Naval Aviation*

F8F-1, BuNo 95364, of VF-20A flies off the flight deck of USS *Boxer* (CV-21) around 1947 or 1948. The letter "B" on the tail and on the wings was the identification code for Carrier Air Group 19. The flaps are extended, and a drop tank is mounted on the centerline pylon. *National Museum of Naval Aviation*

An F8F-1 Bearcat of VF-13 "Aggressors" has crashed into the barricade on USS *Philippine Sea* (CV-47) in September 1949 and is poised, smoke rising from it, ready to fall on its back. In a scenario like this, at best the pilot would survive and the plane could be repaired. In cases of major damage, an aircraft might require extensive repairs, or it might prove beyond salvaging, in which case it would be pushed unceremoniously over the side. At the time of this crash, USS *Philippine Sea* was deployed in the North Atlantic. *National Museum of Naval Aviation*

All five of the Blue Angels' F8F-1 Bearcats were captured in this snapshot taken at an exhibition between 1946 and 1949, although only the tail of "Beetle Bomb" is visible to the left. Each plane had an individual number on the tail, from 0 to 4. *Stan Piet collection*

Only four months after the group was formed, and after having completed four air show performances flying F6F Hellcats, the US Navy flight demonstration team, the Blue Angels, began flying the F8F Bearcat. Initially, the group flew four of the aircraft, while the fifth aircraft was an SNJ trainer, painted yellow and bearing a Japanese rising-sun insignia. During 1949, a fifth F8F replaced the SNJ, and the name "Blue Angels" began to be applied in yellow script on the cowling of the blue Bearcats.

During 1949, the original yellow SNJ "Beetle Bomb" was replaced by F8F-1, BuNo 95187. This aircraft would serve as the solo performer during the Blue Angels demonstrations for the remainder of the group's use of piston-engine-powered aircraft.

The US Navy Blue Angels flew this F8F-1, BuNo 95187, as a solo aircraft during flight demonstrations. Nicknamed "Beetle Bomb," it was painted overall in a glossy orange yellow, with blue lettering. "Beetle Bomb" was written on both sides of the cowl. *Stan Piet collection*

In early January 1949, Ens. Robert E. Tigner of VF-151 at NAS Alameda, California, was flying this F8F-1, BuNo 95346, when a duck collided with the plane, shattering the starboard side of the windshield and the cockpit canopy. The rearview mirror survived. At the top of the instrument panel is the Mk. 8 reflector-type gunsight. Also visible are the top of the control stick grip and the hand crank for operating the sliding canopy. *National Museum of Naval Aviation*

The shattered windshield of Ens. Tigner's F8F-1, BuNo 95346, is viewed from the outside. The collision with the duck also apparently cost the aircraft the clear bubble of its sliding canopy. Visible inside is the pilot's protective back armor and headrest. Tigner later advanced to the rank of commander and was executive officer of VA-56 when he was killed in his A-4C during a training mission in California in 1965. *National Museum of Naval Aviation*

The F8F-1 of the commander of VF-19A prepares for a mission on USS *Boxer* (CV-21) in 1948. During that year, the squadron was on two cruises with USS *Boxer*: April 6 to May 27, and June 25 to August 17. VF-19A was redesignated VF-191 on August 24, 1948. *National Museum of Naval Aviation*

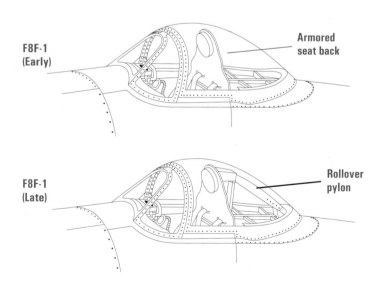

F8F-1
(Early)

Armored
seat back

F8F-1
(Late)

Rollover
pylon

Not all Bearcat pilots were protected by rollover structures. Once rollover protection was developed, it was introduced on the assembly line and was retrofitted to some, but not all, previously delivered aircraft.

Ens. Jesse LeRoy Brown flies an F8F-1B assigned to Ens. Peddy of VF-32. Ens. Brown was the first African American aviator in the US Navy and, ironically, the first KIA naval officer in the Korean War, shot down during the battle of Chosin Reservoir. *National Museum of Naval Aviation*

Grumman F8F-1 Bearcats of Carrier Air Group 19 assemble on the forward end of the flight deck of USS *Boxer* (CV-21) preparatory to launching, somewhere in the western Pacific around 1950. With the exception of the plane to the far left (B 115), which was assigned to VF-191 (formerly VF-19A), these aircraft pertained to VF-192 (formerly VF- 20A). According to instructions for Bearcat pilots, the canopy was to be left open during takeoff but was to be closed before the plane reached a speed of 175 knots. *National Museum of Naval Aviation*

The striped tailhook of F8F-1, BuNo 95000, has just caught the arrestor wire on USS *Cabot* on June 20, 1952, near NAS Pensacola, Florida. The Bearcat was assigned to Carrier Qualification Training Unit 4 (CQTU-4), based at NAS Pensacola. *National Museum of Naval Aviation*

During carrier pilot qualifications on USS *Cabot* (CVL-28) on July 14, 1952, an F8F-1 Bearcat is about to catch the arrestor wire on the flight deck. In the foreground, another wire is poised in case the tailhook of the aircraft fails to catch the first wire. *National Museum of Naval Aviation*

This group of Naval Air Reserve Bearcats was assigned to VF-726 when photographed in July 1952, on the ramp at NAS Glenview, Illinois. The Bearcat equipped several Naval Air Reserve squadrons during the early 1950s. *Stan Piet collection*

US Naval Air Reserve Grumman F8F-1 Bearcats assigned to VF-726, NAS Glenview, Illinois, fly in formation in about 1950. All but the closest plane have orange bands around their fuselages, denoting that they are reserve aircraft. At least the closest three Bearcats, and possibly all four, have practice-bomblet dispensers mounted on pylons under the starboard wings. Each of these dispensers held up to four 25-pound practice bombs, which were much more economical to use in training missions than full-sized bombs. *Stan Piet collection*

An F8F-1 taxis out in preparation for flight. The excellent all-around vision afforded by the bubble top canopy, clearly shown here, was a marked contrast to the razorback configuration of the F8F's predecessor, the F6F. *Stan Piet collection*

The French flew Grumman F8F Bearcats in Indochina during the postwar period. These examples are on recently installed steel matting on the northeast side of the runway at the Tourane Airfield, which later became the Da Nang Air Base. The planes are loaded with napalm bombs. Another Bearcat is parked next to the hangar at the far right.

After the French withdrew from Vietnam in 1954, the Vietnamese air force (VNAF) inherited Bearcats that the French had been using in that country. This F8F-1 was assigned to the 1st Fighter Squadron and wears VNAF markings. *Stan Piet collection*

Photographed in 1948 at the Republic Aviation plant, this F8F-1B, BuNo 122108, wears the "R" tail code of Carrier Air Group 17, and the aircraft number, 104, identifies it as assigned to VF-17. The Bureau Number is just aft of the national insignia on the fuselage. The F8F-1B was similar to the F8F-1 but with four 20 mm cannons installed in the wings instead of four .50-caliber machine guns. *National Museum of Naval Aviation*

The same F8F-1B shown in the preceding photo is viewed from the starboard side. A 100-gallon drop tank is mounted in the centerline rack. Also visible are small whip antennas on the rear deck of the fuselage and on the bottom of the fuselage. *National Museum of Naval Aviation*

Flying near NAS Jacksonville, Florida, in 1949, is F8F-1B, BuNo 95253. The letter "T" code on the tail was that of Carrier Air Group 1. As part of the second squadron in that air group, VF-12 (redesignated from VF-2A in August 1948), the propeller hub, rudder trim tab, and vertical tail top are painted white. *National Museum of Naval Aviation*

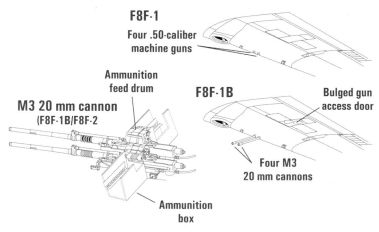

F8F-1
Four .50-caliber machine guns

Ammunition feed drum

M3 20 mm cannon
(F8F-1B/F8F-2

F8F-1B

Bulged gun access door

Four M3 20 mm cannons

Ammunition box

The F8F-1 and F8F-1N had two .50-caliber machine guns per wing, with two hundred rounds for each outboard gun and 325 for each inboard gun. The F8F-1B and F8F-2 and derivatives had two 20 mm cannons per wing, with 188 rounds per outboard cannon and 225 per inboard cannon.

As an F8F-1B of VF-171 (as VF-17 was renamed in August 1948) warms its engine, crewmen rig a catapult bridle to the plane as part of a demonstration of a catapult takeoff at Idlewild Airport (now John F. Kennedy International Airport) on October 23, 1948. *National Museum of Naval Aviation*

The same F8F-1B depicted in the preceding photo takes off, its catapult bridle falling to the ground. This catapult and deck arrangement had been specially constructed to demonstrate the increasingly common use of catapults on Navy aircraft carriers. *National Museum of Naval Aviation*

Recovery is underway on F8F-1B, BuNo 121463, of VF-32 (formerly VF-4A), which flipped over during a landing in wintry conditions at Naval Auxiliary Air Station (NAAS) Charlestown, Rhode Island, in 1949. *National Museum of Naval Aviation*

On January 19, 1945, Lt. j.g. Levio E. Zeni's F8F-1B, BuNo 121469, of VF-33, is out of control during a landing on USS *Leyte* (CV-32). Its starboard wingtip was severed when it struck the 5-inch gun mount to the right and is airborne above the plane. *National Museum of Naval Aviation*

The fuselage of F8F-1B, BuNo 121469, is fully engulfed in flames, and the engine supports have collapsed as Lt. j.g. Zeni struggles to extricate himself from the cockpit. *To the bottom left,* a firefighter rushes to help put out the flames. Although the plane was a total loss, Zeni survived the accident. Visible on top of each wing are two blisters to provide clearance to the 20 mm cannons housed inside the wings. *National Museum of Naval Aviation*

Crewmen manhandle an F8F-1B of VF-16A (redesignated VF-152 in July 1948) on the deck of a fleet carrier. The man to the right guides the tailwheel by using a tow bar, while the crewman next to the port main landing-gear strut is holding a wheel chock. The two streamlined blisters to give clearance to the 20 mm cannons are visible on top of the port wing. *Naval History and Heritage Command*

When the port main landing gear failed on F8F-1N, BuNo 95320, of Night Development Squadron 1 (VCN-1) on the night of November 15, 1947, the plane was destroyed on the deck of USS *Valley Forge* (CV-45), but the pilot, Lt. F. S. Moody, was not injured. *Grumman Memorial Park via Leo Polaski*

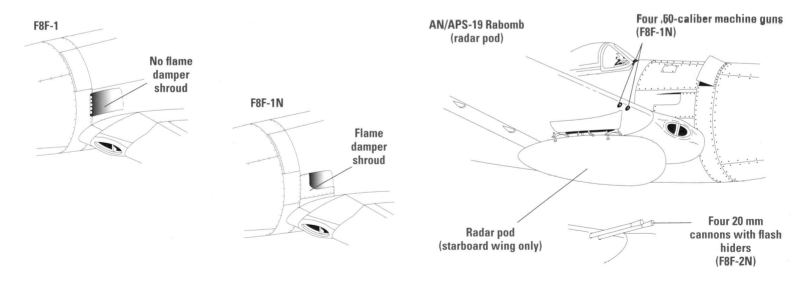

In order to mask the visibility of the aircraft in night skies, as well as to preserve the pilot's night vision, the F8F-1N was equipped with flame-dampening shrouds on the exhaust stubs.

The proximity of the wing hinge to the fuselage prevented the radar system from being embedded in the wing, as it was on Hellcat night fighters. Rather, it was suspended beneath the starboard wing.

F8F-1, BuNo 90446 and civil registration NL14HP, was owned by Howard Pardue's Breckenridge Aviation Museum, Breckenridge, Texas. Pardue's F8F was the oldest example of the Bearcat existent, being one of the original twenty-three evaluation aircraft. Sadly, Pardue was killed and this aircraft destroyed in a crash at their home field on April 4, 2012. The name "Kimberly Brooke" is on the cowl below the red-and-white stripes. Kimberly Brooke was Pardue's daughter, who had preceded him in death. The sliding canopy has the tilted rear frame associated with the F8F-2. The pitot tube is visible under the wing. *Rich Kolasa*

Pardue's aircraft had been transferred to the National Air and Space Museum in 1952. In 1976, it was traded to Darryl Greenamyer for his world-record-setting F8F-2 Conquest I. The aircraft subsequently found its way into Pardue's hands. *Rich Kolasa*

The port wing-fold joint of a Bearcat is viewed from the front. Protruding from the rib that forms the edge of the outboard wing section are two lugs, each with a hole through it. These lugs are locked to the inboard wing section when the wing is extended.

The port wing-fold joint of a Bearcat is viewed from the side. The light-colored rod is the aileron control rod. Directly above the forward end of that rod is the aft wing hinge. The forward hinge is above the green tube farther forward on the wing rib.

The port wing-fold joint is viewed from aft of the inboard port wing, with the folded outboard section of the wing to the top center and the aileron to the top left. The white area on the outboard wing section is part of the national insignia.

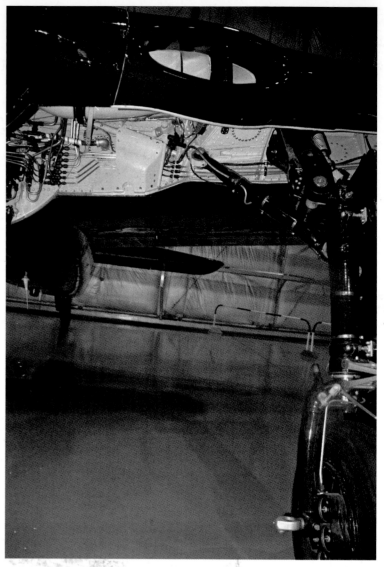

The port main landing gear is observed from the front, showing how snugly the main strut door fits against the main oleo strut and tire. A tie-down/towing eye can be seen on the inboard side of the axle. Above the tire is the forward-pointing antitorque link, sometimes also called the scissors. Also in view on the leading edge of the wing is the split air intake for engine induction and for the left oil cooler.

More of the port main landing gear is shown, with a good view of the trunnion assembly above the top of the oleo strut. The blue, angled rod connected to the oleo strut and to the rear of the landing-gear bay is the drag link, which acted to raise the oleo strut and wheel as the trunnion was retracted. The main spar of the wing also forms the rear bulkhead of the main landing-gear bay. Arrayed on the spar are various hydraulic lines.

The part of the main landing gear below the antitorque link (visible at the top of the photo) is called the half fork; the port one is viewed from the inboard side. At the bottom of the half fork is the axle. The tie-down/towing eye is clearly visible on the side of the axle. Forward of the half fork is the hydraulic brake assembly. Below the antitorque link is a link connecting the main oleo strut with the main strut door.

The port main landing-gear bay is viewed facing inboard, with the starboard wheel visible below the open door at the inboard edge of the landing-gear bay. At the top left is the hydraulic operating cylinder for the landing gear. The horizontal ring below the piston rod of the cylinder is a tie-down eye. Below the eye is the drag link for the oleo strut. Elements of the engine accessory compartment are visible at the far end of the bay.

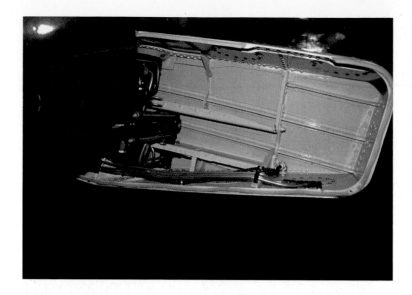

At the top left of this view of the outboard part of the port main landing-gear bay is the top of the main landing-gear strut door, adjacent to which is the hydraulic cylinder that operates the main landing gear.

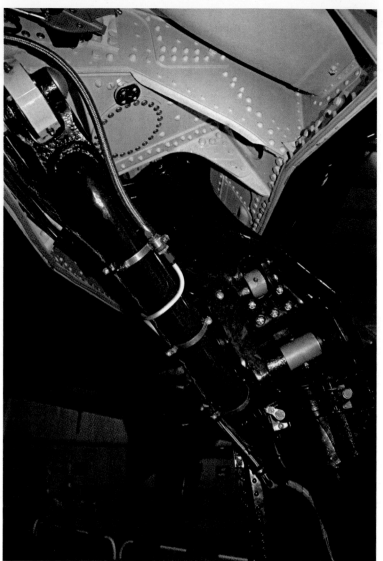

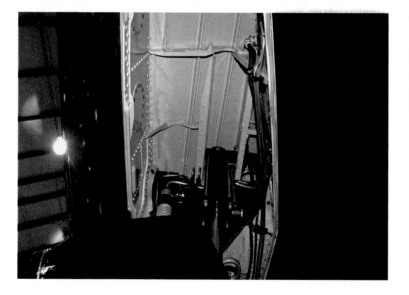

The outboard portion of the port main landing-gear bay is observed from a slightly different angle than in the photo above, with the leading edge of the wing to the left. The top of the operating cylinder for the main landing gear is pinned to the two angle brackets on the roof of the landing-gear bay, enabling the cylinder to pivot as the landing-gear strut is retracted or lowered.

In this view facing outboard, running diagonally across the photo is the port main landing-gear drag link, with a hydraulic line secured to it. The top of the drag link is secured with a pin to a mounting bracket. To the right is the main landing-gear trunnion, while at the bottom right is the top of the port oleo strut. Details of the interior of the landing-gear bay are also visible, including the riveted construction of the bracing.

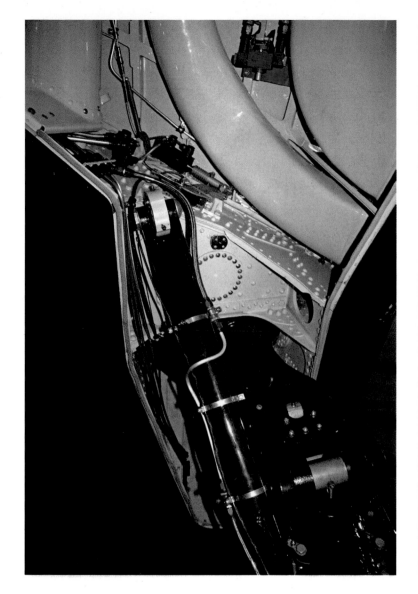

Like in the preceding photograph, this view is looking up at the port main landing-gear bay. This view incorporates more of the inboard part of the bay, however. The rounded structure at the top right corner is part of the oil-cooler air intake. To the left of that intake, the curved object is the induction-air intake.

Visible through the inboard side of the port main landing-gear bay is the engine accessory compartment, between the engine and the cockpit. At the top left is the oil-cooler air duct, and the brass-colored drum below it is the left oil-cooler assembly. To the upper right is the induction-air duct.

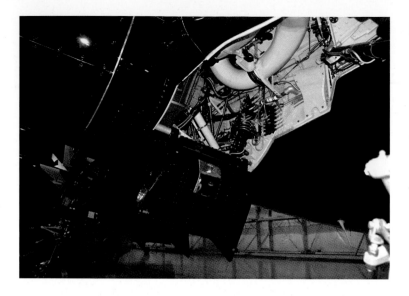

The inboard portion of the port main landing-gear bay of an F8F-1 is viewed, with the underside of the engine cowl to the left, and the curved shape of the induction duct is at the top of the landing-gear bay. Hydraulic and fuel lines are also in evidence.

The open main landing-gear-wheel doors, mounted on the fuselage belly along the longitudinal centerline of the Bearcat, are observed facing aft. Between the doors are the oil-cooler air-exit duct shutters. These were redesigned for the F8F-2.

The port rear of the fuselage of an F8F-1 is exhibited, along with a view of part of its tail landing gear. Two circular, flush-fitting access panels are fastened to the fuselage. Above the nomenclature stencil "F8F-1" is the plane's civil registration, NL9G.

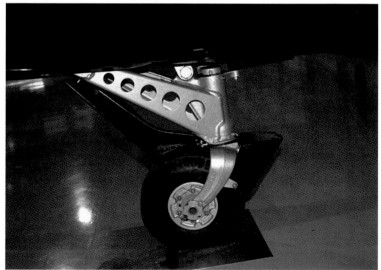

The tail landing gear of an F8F-1 is swiveled 180 degrees aft. Attached to the front of the landing-gear strut is a small, blue-painted door, which closed off the opening when the gear was retracted. An even-smaller fairing is attached to the wheel yoke.

The tail landing-gear strut, as seen from the rear, comprises a pivoting arm assembly with lightening holes in the sides and a vertical socket welded to the rear of it to accept the swiveling yoke for the tailwheel. The wheel well opening is also in view.

This view of the port side of an F8F-1's empennage—that is, the vertical and horizontal tail surfaces and controls—reveals that the leading edge of the elevator has a rounded contour, similar to that of a wing. The outlines of the ribs of the elevator are discernible through their fabric skin. Also discernible is a slot in the leading edge of the elevator to provide clearance for the outboard hinge of the elevator.

This F8F-1, BuNo 90454, is viewed from below in flight. Two oil-cooler air-outlet shutters are visible on the bottom of the fuselage aft of the cowl. There is a slight swelling on the wings around the ram-air intakes. *Brian Lockett*

Some sixty years after it left the Grumman assembly line, F8F-1, BuNo 90454, currently civil registration NL9G, taxis to a runway for one more takeoff. The angled antenna aft of the open canopy appears to be a recent addition instead of original equipment. *Brian Lockett*

Howard Pardue's Bearcat, BuNo 90446, was the tenth production F8F-1 to roll off Grumman's production line. His Breckenridge Aviation Museum acquired the plane in 1984, and he flew it in many events, including the National Air Races. *Rich Kolasa*

F8F-1, BuNo 90454, now civil registration NL9G, was the eighteenth production F8F, to which Grumman assigned construction number D.18. It is shown with an F8F-2-type canopy with a slanted rear frame. The white antenna aft of the canopy is nonoriginal equipment. *Brian Lockett*

Wings folded, F8F-1, BuNo 90454, is observed from the front. A good view is provided of the Aeroproducts propeller, complete with company logo on each blade. Jutting down from the wings at the wing-fold joints are the levers for operating the wing locks. *Brian Lockett*

CHAPTER 2
F8F-2

In 1948, the F8F-1 aircraft gave way to the F8F-2, which, in addition to coming with the four 20 mm cannon, also featured a taller vertical stabilizer and was powered by an R-2800-34W engine with water injection. F8F-1 BuNo 95049 and F8F-1B BuNo 95330 served as prototypes for the improved design. The true XF8F-2 first flew on June 11, 1947, with Carl Alber at the controls. Suitably impressed, the Navy ordered that the F8F-2 replace the F8F-1 on Grumman production lines. Beyond the 365 basic F8F-2 Bearcats, twelve F8F-2N night-fighter variants and sixty camera-carrying F8F-2P photoreconnaissance variants were built.

Efforts to create a photoreconnaissance version of the Bearcat began early in the F8F program, when the fifth development aircraft, BuNo 90441, was modified by the Naval Aircraft Factory into reconnaissance configuration. This 1946 conversion would produce the only F8F-1P. Grumman, however, factory-assembled sixty of the F8F- 2P aircraft between February 1948 and May 1949. The camera installations in the rear fuselage cavity on the Grumman-built aircraft replicated those trialed in 1946 by the Naval Aircraft Factory. Both vertical and oblique mountings were provided for K-17 or K-18 aerial cameras.

The K-17 was a 9-by-9-inch format (negative size) camera used for reconnaissance and mapping. It had 6-, 12-, and 24-inch focal-length options. The K-18 was a 9-by-18-inch-format camera with a 24-inch focal length. Both types of cameras were made by the Fairchild Camera and Instrument Company and used Eastman Aerial Safety film, which came in rolls either 75 or 200 feet long and 9½ inches wide. It has been reported that additional Bearcats were modified to F8F-2P standards by the fleet, although no definitive documents supporting these reports have yet surfaced.

Rather than the usual four M3 20 mm cannons, mounted two per wing, the F8F-2P carried only a single such weapon in each wing. This change shaved about 500 pounds from the aircraft's weight, making the camera planes among the fastest of the Bearcats. The F8F-2P was assigned to squadron VC-61 in the Pacific Fleet and VC-62 in the Atlantic Fleet. The squadrons provided a detachment for each of the carrier air wings in the fleets.

Grumman delivered the final F8F-2 in April 1949.

Despite its impressive time-to-climb capabilities, Navy trials against a P-80 in 1946 showed the jet to have clear performance advantages. The Bearcat equipped a total of twenty-four Navy and Marine Corps squadrons. Among those was the prestigious Blue Angels flight demonstration team, who flew the Bearcat from 1946 through 1950.

Surplus Bearcats were supplied to the Royal Thai Air Force and the French Armée de l'Air, which then passed them along to the South Vietnamese air force. The F8F was out of frontline US Navy service prior to the onset of the Korean War, since the Corsair was preferred in the close-air-support role. Once relegated to surplus, the Bearcat was popular on the air-race circuit, with a few continuing in the role today.

A test pilot takes a newly minted F8F-2 for a flight over Long Island in 1948. On the engine cowl is Grumman's temporary aircraft number, in the factory's distinctive style. This number was the last three digits of the plane's Bureau Number, 121612. The principal visible feature differentiating the F8F-2 from the preceding F8F-1 was the vertical fin and rudder, which were 12 inches taller than the vertical fin and rudder on the F8F-1. In addition, on the F8F-2 the rudder trim tab was positioned higher than on the F8F-1, and the trim tab protruded slightly to the rear of the trailing edge of the rudder. Two 20 mm cannons instead of two .50-caliber machine guns were in each wing, with two blisters in the access door over the cannon receivers on each wing. There were other changes in the F8F-2 that were not so discernible. *National Museum of the United States Air Force*

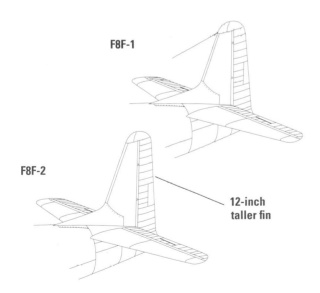

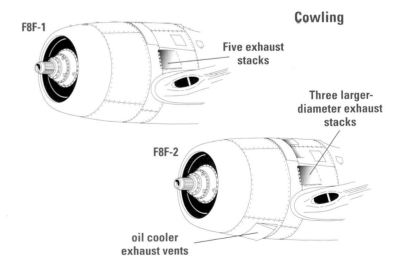

A key feature for differentiating between the F8F-1 and F8F-2 is the taller vertical stabilizer and rudder of the F8F-2, which were 12 inches taller than those of the F8F-1, in order to compensate for the increased torque of the F8F-2's R-2800-30W engine.

The F8F-1 Bearcat had five small exhaust stacks per side, while the F8F-2 replaced these with three larger exhausts on each side. The F8F-2 also introduced two oil-cooler air-exit shutters on the underside of the engine cowling that had not been present on the F8F-1.

F8F-2, BuNo 121546, bears the letter "L" code on its vertical tail and under the port wing, indicating it was assigned to Carrier Air Group 7. The white propeller hub and vertical tail tip signify that the plane was the second squadron in the group: that is, VF-72. *National Museum of Naval Aviation*

An F8F-2 of VF-73 is being readied for a catapult launch on USS *Princeton* (CV-32) in 1948. This squadron was established in July 1947, and its Bearcats had unique, diagonal flashes with blue squadron colors on the upper fronts of their vertical stabilizers. *National Museum of Naval Aviation*

Poised ready for a catapult launch on USS *Coral Sea* (CVB-43) on September 14, 1948, this F8F-2 served with VF-62, and the "C" code pertained to Carrier Air Group 6. The squadron was undertaking a short training cruise. The squadron insignia is on the cowl. *National Museum of Naval Aviation*

Deck crewmen hunker down in front of Grumman F8F-1s of VF-71 while other crewmen prepare to remove the wheel chocks on USS *Leyte* (CV-32) on March 9, 1949. In the background are a number of Grumman TBM Avenger torpedo bombers. *National Museum of Naval Aviation*

Several F8F-2s are being readied for launching from USS *Valley Forge* (CV-45) in September 1949. The first two Bearcats are BuNos 121746 and 121722. Under the left wing of the first plane is a practice-bomblet dispenser. The occasion evidently was a VIP event, judging by the numerous civilians observing from the island.

During a 1949 North Atlantic cruise, the flight deck chief of USS *Franklin D. Roosevelt* (CVB-42) watches at the center as the flight deck officer to the right gives a hand signal to the pilot of a Grumman F8F-2 assigned to VF-61 "Jolly Rogers." *National Museum of Naval Aviation*

Grumman F8F-2 Bearcats of VF-61 "Jolly Rogers" were photographed on the flight deck of USS *Franklin D. Roosevelt* (CVB-42) in 1949. The squadron's insignia, a Jolly Roger pirate flag with skull and crossbones, is visible on the engine cowlings. *National Museum of Naval Aviation*

An F8F-2 of VF-151 is being hoisted to the flight deck of USS *Boxer* at NAS Alameda, California, on January 10, 1950. Another Bearcat is in the foreground, with more lined up in the background adjacent to Douglas Skyraiders. San Francisco is in the distance. *Grumman Memorial Park via Leo Polaski*

From January 11, 1950, through June 13, 1950, VF-151 flew F8F-2 Bearcats from USS *Boxer* (CV-21) while operating in the western Pacific. The unit was redesignated VF-192 on February 15, 1950.

A mobile dockside crane handles a Grumman Bearcat of Carrier Air Group 15 during an aircraft-carrier transfer operation. The white area at the top of the vertical tail of the Bearcat suspended from the boom suggests that the aircraft was detailed to VF-16A or, as it was redesignated in July 1948, VF-152. The Skyraider resting on the dock is marked with the letter "B," designator for Carrier Air Group 19, and has what appears to be an APS-4 radar pod on the pylon under the port wing. *Naval History and Heritage Command*

Bearcats warm their engines preparatory to a mission. The F8F-1 in the foreground was assigned to VF-72, as indicated by the air-group code "R" and the white propeller hub and vertical tail tip. The crewmen walking by the landing gears carry wheel chocks. *National Museum of Naval Aviation*

This US Marine Corps F8F-2 marked number 537 is armed with two subcaliber aircraft rockets (SCAR), used for rocketry practice, under each wing, and one practice-bomblet dispenser mounted on the bomb / drop tank pylon under the starboard wing.

Clearly visible are the wing-fold joint and mechanisms on this F8F-2, BuNo 122626, of VF-62. The rod set at an angle along the joint is the actuator for the aileron. On the engine cowl is the squadron's insignia: a skeletal cowboy riding a rocket. *National Museum of Naval Aviation*

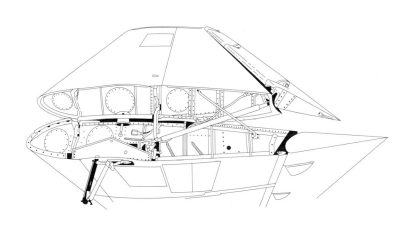

Compared with the swing-back wing-fold mechanism of the Bearcat's Grumman-built predecessors, the F4F and F6F, the Bearcat's wing-fold design was a model of simplicity, with two hinges and a locking system enabling the wings to be manually folded inward.

The US Marine Corps employed Grumman Bearcats as advanced trainers in 1951 and 1952 at Marine Corps Air Station (MCAS) Quantico, Virginia; Cherry Point, North Carolina; and El Toro, California. These two F8F-2s served at MCAS Quantico. *USMC*

F8F-2P, BuNo 121660, of Composite Squadron 62 (VC-62) "Shutter Bugs," sits on a tarmac at NAS Norfolk, Virginia, on May 23, 1950. The F8F-2P carried a vertical camera aft of the cockpit and an oblique camera with sliding door aft of the port wing root. The sliding door was partially enclosed by a C-shaped fairing designed to deflect oil and dirt from the camera door. A deflector was also available for the vertical camera door on the bottom of the fuselage. *National Museum of Naval Aviation*

Sailors inspect F8F-2P, BuNo121735, assigned to VC-62. An oblique camera door and fairing were not installed on this side of the fuselage aft of the wing, and F8F-2Ps carried only two 20 mm cannons, in the inboard positions. Various combinations of K-17 and K-18 cameras could be installed in the vertical and oblique positions. Much of the VC-62 squadron insignia on the side of the engine cowl has chipped off. One prototype and sixty production F8F-2Ps were delivered. *National Museum of Naval Aviation*

Grumman F8F-2P, BuNo 121737, of VC-62 flies alongside a coastal mountain range around 1950. This plane made a forced water landing alongside USS *Coral Sea* (CVB-43) on July 1, 1951. The pilot was rescued and survived the ditching in fine shape. *National Museum of Naval Aviation*

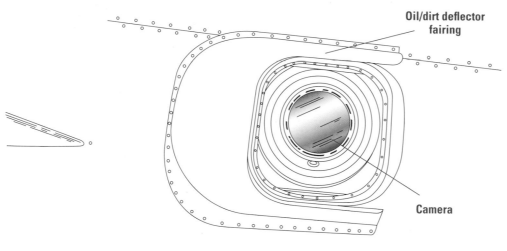

Oil/dirt deflector fairing

Camera

Lower oil/dirt deflector plate for vertical camera

The oblique camera door and oil-and-dirt deflector of the F8F-2P is immediately aft of the trailing edge of the port wing, which is shown to the left. The sliding door is shown open. On the bottom of the fuselage, slightly forward of the oblique camera door, is the oil-and-dirt deflector for the vertical camera.

An F8F-2P assigned to Composite Squadron 62 (VC-62) "Shutterbugs" flies high above the clouds near NAS Norfolk, Virginia, in 1948. A close examination of the photograph discloses that on the bottom of the fuselage, below the number 12 on the side of the cockpit, is the slightly raised deflector that prevented dirt and oil from smearing the window for the vertical camera. Below the cowl, an oil-cooler air-exit shutter is hanging open. *National Museum of Naval Aviation*

Three Bearcats of VC-61, including F8F-2P, BuNo 121583, *in the foreground*, fly in formation on April 1, 1949. Activated on January 1, 1949, Composite Squadron 61 was based at NAS Miramar, California, and performed photoreconnaissance duties for the Pacific Fleet. Bearcats of this squadron were deployed six separate times with Pacific Fleet aircraft carriers between July 1949 and June 1950. *National Museum of Naval Aviation*

Ships of Task Force 201, including USS *Leyte* (CV-32), cruise below as a Grumman F8F-2P passes overhead in September 1951. The squadron insignia is just below the front of the cockpit's windshield. Such insignia were limited in size to 6 inches square. The large "PL" on the vertical stabilizer denotes Photo Atlantic Fleet. Pacific Fleet photo aircraft carried PP markings on the vertical stabilizer, as seen in the photo at left. *National Museum of Naval Aviation*

Two F8F-2Ps marked PL-20 and PL-18, assigned to VC-62, warm their engines on the flight deck of USS *Oriskany* (CV-34) in the Mediterranean in 1951. Each of the F8F-2Ps carries a drop tank under each wing. In the background are Douglas Skyraiders. *National Museum of Naval Aviation*

A number of Grumman Bearcats served as demonstration and racing aircraft, such as this one nicknamed the Red Ship that Grumman fabricated from an F8F-2 airframe and surplus parts and used as a demonstrator. Powered by an R-2800-34W engine and assigned the Grumman model number G-58B, this aircraft was built for use by Roger Wolfe Kahn. The head of the Grumman Service Department, Kahn used this aircraft in the same manner he had previously used F6F Hellcats—to visit squadrons flying Grumman-built aircraft as needed for training or troubleshooting purposes. The drop tank was modified to carry small cargo items, tools, and spare parts. Sometimes also referred to as the "Red Job," the Red Ship survives at the Planes of Fame Air Museum. *National Museum of the United States Air Force*

This colorful civil Bearcat began life as F8F-2P, BuNo 121608. Bill Fornof, a Cadillac-Oldsmobile dealer from Houma, Louisiana, owned and flew the Bearcat, which he had painted in colors taken from Cadillac automobiles. The aircraft and pilot were lost in an accident at Quonset, Rhode Island, on June 5, 1971, when metal fatigue led to a wing failure before 75,000 spectators.

F8F Series Data

	XF8F-1	F8F-1	F8F-1B	F8F-1N	F8F-2	F8F-2N	F8F-2P
First delivery	2/26/45	12/30/44	2/27/46	5/29/46	10/11/47	11/21/47	2/20/48
Last delivery	2/26/45	8/29/47	1/28/48	11/12/46	4/14/49	4/22/49	5/31/49
Engine, P&W	R-2800-22W	R-2800-34W	R-2800-34W	R-2800-34W	R-2800-30W	R-2800-30W	R-2800-30W
Armament	4 x .50-cal.	4 x .50-cal.	4 x 20 mm	4 x 50-cal	4 x 20 mm	4 x 20 mm	2 x 20 mm
Wingspan	35', 6"	35', 6"	35', 6"	35', 6"	35', 6"	35', 6"	35', 6"
Span, folded	23', 3"	23', 3"	23', 3"	23', 3"	23', 3"	23', 3"	23', 3"
Length	27', 6"	27', 6"	27', 6"	27', 6"	27', 6"	27', 6"	27', 6"
Height on gear	13', 8"	13', 8"	13', 8"	13', 8"	13', 8"	13', 8"	13', 8"
Weight empty	7,017 lbs.	7,170 lbs.	7,216 lbs .	7,510 lbs.	7,650 lbs.	7,775 lbs.	8,125 lbs.
Combat weight	8,116 lbs.	9,334 lbs.	9,672 lbs.	9,770 lbs.	10,337 lbs.	10,100 lbs.	10,080 lbs.
Max speed	455 mph	429 mph	372 mph	419 mph	388 mph	385 mph	388 mph
Max Climb, fpm	6,500	5,600	5,610	5,550	4,465	4,360	4,570
Ferry range	1,450 miles	1,965 miles	1,810 miles	1,895 miles	1,595 miles	1,586 miles	1,595 miles
Service ceiling	41,300 ft.	38,900 ft.	34,800 ft.	34,900 ft.	38,200 ft.	40,500 ft.	38,350 ft.
Internal fuel	162 gals.	185 gals.	185 gals.	185 gals.	185 gals.	185 gals.	185 gals.

Bearcat Bureau Numbers:

2	XF8F-1:90460–90461
23	Pre-production F8F-1: 90437–90459
747	F8F-1: 94752–95498
1	F8F-1B prototype converted from F8F-1: 94972
98	F8F-1B conversions from F8F-1: 94982, 94987, 94999, 95002, 95009, 95015, 95022, 95028, 95033, 95039, 95044, 95050, 95056, 95062, 95068, 95074, 95080, 95086, 95093, 95098, 95103, 95108, 95113, 95118, 95123, 95128, 95133, 95138, 95143, 95148, 95156, 95162, 95166, 95172, 95176, 95181, 95190, 95195, 95200, 95205, 95210, 95215, 95221, 95227, 95232, 95237, 95242, 95247, 95253, 95260, 95265, 95271, 95275, 95281, 95285, 95290, 95295, 95300, 95305, 95310, 95315, 95319, 95324, 95334, 95340, 95344, 95349, 95354, 95359, 95363, 95368, 95373, 95378, 95383, 95387, 95391, 95396, 95401, 95406, 95411, 95416, 95420, 95425, 95430, 95435, 95440, 95445, 95450, 95454, 95459, 95463, 95468, 95472, 95477, 95482, 95487, 95492, 95498
126	F8F-1B: 121463–121522 and 122087–122152
1	F8F-1C prototype converted from F8F-1: 94803
1	F8F-1D prototype converted from F8F-1: 90456
13	F8F-1D converted from F8F-1: 90446, 90447, 90451–90457, 94752, 95009, 95325, 95342
1	F8F-1E prototype converted from F8F-1: 90445
2	XF8F-1N prototype converted from: 94812 and 94819
12	F8F-1N: 95034, 95140, 95150, 95161, 95171, 95184, 95191, 95198, 95206, 95214, 95222, 95230
1	F8F-1P prototype converted from F8F-1: 90441
2	XF8F-2 prototype converted from F8F-1s: 95049, 95330
365	F8F-2: 121523–121792 and 122614–122708
1	F8F-2N: prototype converted from F8F-2: 121549
12	F8F-2N converted from F8F-2: 121549–121550, 121575–121579, 121601–121605
1	F8F-2P prototype converted from F8F-2: 121580
60	F8F-2P converted from F8F-2s: 121580–121585, 121606–121611, 121632–121637, 121658–121663, 121684–121689, 121709–121714, 121734–121739, 121758–121763, 121770–121775, 121785–121790

A handful of Bearcats survive, including this fine example of an F8F-2 in the collections of the Southern California Wing of the Commemorative Air Force, Camarillo, California. The plane is BuNo 122674 and currently is assigned civil registration number N7825C. It is shown in markings for VF-6A of Carrier Air Group 5. On the engine cowl is the arrowhead-shaped insignia of VF-6A. *Rich Kolasa*

F8F-2, BuNo 121748 and civil registration NX1DF, displays its forward port side. Above the three engine exhausts is the open port cowl flap. The positioning of the unpainted metal fasteners for the cowl panels is clearly visible. Marked in white on the bottom of the main landing-gear door are recommendations for the tire pressure of the main tires: 105 psi normal and 165 psi maximum. *Rich Kolasa*

The inner parts of the propeller blades, the propeller hub, and part of the front of the engine, particularly the gear-reduction casing, are viewed close-up on an F8F-2. Blade serial number, assembly number, and high and low pitch angles are marked on the blades. *Stan Piet collection*

The Aeroproducts constant-speed propeller assembly on F8F-1, BuNo 90454, includes four blades, assembly number H20F-162-11M5, and a hub containing the hydraulically controlled propeller pitch-adjusting mechanism. The cap on the hub is attached with twelve hex fasteners, with a locking wire wrapped around the fasteners in threes. Some details of the front of the Pratt & Whitney R-2800 radial engine are also visible. *Stan Piet collection*

The underside of the folded port wing of F8F-2P Bearcat, BuNo 121710, at the National Museum of Naval Aviation is displayed. Between the letters "N" and "A" in "Navy" is a pitot tube. The stencil to the top of the wing indicates where to insert the bar for folding and unfolding the wing. The wings were constructed of aluminum alloy skin over metal frames. The ailerons were formed from metal frames with fabric skin over them.

Seen up close is the wing-fold joint on F8F-2P, BuNo 121710, at the National Museum of Naval Aviation. Above the front and the rear of the triangular piece with the three lightening holes at the bottom of the joint is a wing-fold hinge.

The propeller and cowl of the F8F-2P at the National Museum of Naval Aviation are observed from the port side. The Aeroproducts constant-speed propellers used on Bearcats were 12'7" in diameter and housed a pitch-changing mechanism in the hub.

Part of the port main landing gear and bay are in view. Above and aft of the top of the main strut door is a hydraulic operating cylinder. A red cover has been stuffed into the induction/oil-cooler air intake on the leading edge of the wing. Exhausts are also visible. *Rich Kolasa*

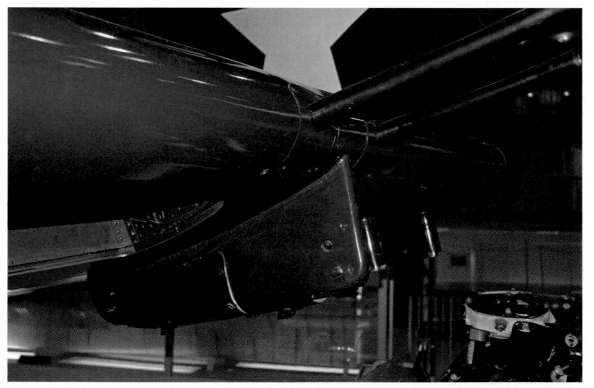

Two 20 mm cannons protrude over the bomb or drop-tank pylon on the port wing of the National Museum of Naval Aviation's F8F-2P. In actuality, the F8F-2P photoreconnaissance Bearcat had only one 20 mm cannon per wing, in the inboard position.

Because of considerations of the length and positioning of the main landing-gear struts, the top of each strut was mounted on an outward-swiveling articulated trunnion, making for a longer landing gear when lowered and a shorter landing gear when retracted.

The cockpit canopy of the F8F-2 of the Commemorative Air Force is observed from the port side. The angled frame on the aft part of the clear blister of the sliding canopy was introduced partway through production of the F8F-2 and was not present on the F8F-1. *Rich Kolasa*

F8F-2, BuNo 121748 and civil registration NX1DF, is currently piloted by Dan Friedkin and bears the "D" tail code of a Bearcat in Carrier Air Group 9. The diagonal white line aft of the aircraft number 224 on the fuselage was a visual aid to help pilots and crewmen locate the recessed step at the bottom of the line and the recessed handhold at the top of the line. A noticeable feature of the F8F-2 and its derivatives, in addition to the tall vertical tail, is that the trim tab juts slightly aft of the trailing edge of the rudder. *Rich Kolasa*

The nearest Bearcat, flying in close formation with F8F-2, BuNo 121748 (D-224), is F8F-2, BuNo 122637, bearing the "F" tail code of Carrier Air Group 4. The tips of the vertical tails of both planes are red; in the late 1940s this signified the first squadron in the group, although these aircraft carry the modexes of aircraft in the second squadron. *Rich Kolasa*

The two F8F-2s in the preceding photograph are displayed inside a hangar. US Navy Bearcats were normally painted overall Glossy Sea Blue. In actual service, the glossy paint quickly weathered to a duller sheen than the mirrorlike paint on these two planes. *Rich Kolasa*

F8F-2, BuNo 122619, has been restored with markings of a Bearcat serving with the Naval Air Reserve at NAS Denver, Colorado, from 1949 to the early 1950s. The angled frame toward the rear of the sliding canopy was introduced with the F8F-2. *Rich Kolasa*

The F8F-2P at the National Museum of Naval Aviation, BuNo 121710, is viewed from its aft port quarter. It features a reproduction of one of the more ornate Bearcat markings schemes, that of Cmdr. E. E. Cook Jr., commander of Carrier Air Group 19. *Rich Kolasa*

F8F-2, BuNo 121748, piloted by Dan Friedkin, displays its empennage, including the "D" tail code used by aircraft of Carrier Air Group 9 in the late 1940s. During that time period, Bearcats of several squadrons sometimes had the horizontal red and yellow stripes on the rudder trim tabs and tails. When a carrier air group color was applied to the top of the vertical stabilizer and rudder (i.e., red for the first squadron and white for the second), it was to be 7 inches in height. *Rich Kolasa*

The trim tab of an F8F-2 is seen from the port side. The leading edge of the tab is sharply angled rather than rounded. The top and bottom corners of the trailing edge of the tab are rounded. Unlike the rudder, which consisted of fabric skin over a metal frame, the trim tab was fabricated with an aluminum alloy skin over a metal frame. This photo illustrates how the rear of the rudder trim tab extended aft of the trailing edge of the rudder. *Stan Piet collection*

The rudder and vertical stabilizer of an F8F-2 are viewed close-up. When the heights of the vertical stabilizer and the rudder were increased by 12 inches starting with the F8F-2, this change resulted in an increase in the vertical stabilizer's area from 20.8 square feet to 22.5 square feet and an increase in the rudder and trim-tab area from 8.1 square feet to 8.16 square feet. The width and area of the horizontal stabilizers and elevators remained the same in the various production models of the Bearcat. *Rich Kolasa*

A 150-gallon drop tank is mounted on the centerline pylon underneath the fuselage of F8F-2P, BuNo 121710, at the National Museum of Naval Aviation, Pensacola, Florida. The aircraft, viewed here from starboard, features considerable white stenciling. The hook assembly of the tailhook is at the aft end of the fuselage below the red and white stripes. The pilot extended the tailhook using a T-handle on the floor to the left of his seat. *Rich Kolasa*

The starboard horizontal stabilizer, elevator, and trim tab are viewed close-up. Fabric-covered control surfaces were used because their lower mass, compared with metal-covered control surfaces, delayed the onset of control-surface flutter.

Like the rudder, the elevators of the F8F-2P are formed of doped fabric stretched over metal frames. The locations of the ribs of the elevator frame show through the fabric skin on this aircraft at the National Museum of Naval Aviation. In this view of the starboard side of the vertical stabilizer and rudder as well as the starboard horizontal stabilizer and elevator, the trim tab is toward the center of the trailing edge of each elevator.

The castering tailwheel is turned toward the rear of the aircraft in this starboard-side view of the National Museum of Naval Aviation's F8F-2P. Like the main landing gear, the tail landing gear was hydraulically operated by the pilot in conjunction with the main landing gear.

At the extreme rear of the fuselage of F8F-2P Bearcat, BuNo 121710, at the National Museum of Naval Aviation, is a small, white stencil reading "jack point." The words marked a spot for securing a jack for raising the tail of the aircraft.

The stressed skin of the Bearcats' semimonocoque fuselage was formed from thick 302W aluminum alloy. The skin was fastened to the frame by flush rivets and spot-welding, resulting in a very smooth surface with hard-to-detect seams.

The raised ridges on the starboard elevator indicate where the ribs of the elevator frame are located. The seams of the fabric covering are also discernible, as are the rivets on the trim tab that fasten the metal skin to the frame. The span of the horizontal stabilizer is 189 inches.

Below the sliding canopy and fastened to the rear of the pilot's armor is the rollover crash-protection arch, which worked like a roll bar should the plane flip over on landing. The canopy is formed of ¼-inch Plexiglas mounted on an aluminum-alloy frame. The pilot operated the canopy with a hand crank inside the cockpit. Pressing a button below the starboard side of the windshield opened the canopy from the outside. *Rich Kolasa*

The starboard side of the fuselage around the cockpit, along with the forward part of the fuselage and other features, is in view. To the left is the white diagonal line that helped the pilot discern the recessed step at the bottom and the recessed handhold at the top—features that would otherwise have been hard to find quickly in darkness or even in the daytime, given the dark color of the Glossy Sea Blue paint. The bare-metal panel on the fuselage aft of the engine exhausts, often seen on surviving Bearcats, normally would have been painted Glossy Sea Blue during the planes' original service. *Rich Kolasa*

Seen here up close from starboard, this F8F-2P at the National Museum of Naval Aviation features reproduction markings for the commander of Air Group 19. White "no step" and "no push" caution markings are on the starboard flap. The fin-type antenna atop the aft part of the fuselage of the F8F-2P at the National Museum of Naval Aviation is not original-issue equipment. Originally, a whip antenna would have been present in this area. Next to the antenna is a teardrop-shaped formation light.

More of the starboard aileron of the same F8F-2P shown in the preceding photo appears here, along with the inboard part of the aileron and trim tab on the folded part of the wing. Two blisters for 20 mm cannons are visible on an access panel on top of the wing, despite the fact that the F8F-2P reconnaissance aircraft had only one cannon in each wing while in service.

Two cannon barrels protrude from the starboard wing of the F8F-2P at the National Museum of Naval Aviation at Pensacola. Original F8F-2Ps had only one 20 mm cannon in each wing, in the inboard position, two cannons being omitted to save weight.

F8F-2, BuNo 121748, waits on a runway at an air show as F-F/A-18 Hornets of the US Navy's Blue Angels fly in a four-plane diamond formation overhead. The Blue Angels flew five F8F-1s from 1946 to mid-1949: four for formation flying and one for solo flying. Fittingly, it was Bearcat pilots flying under the command of LCDR Bob Clarke who pioneered the Blue Angels' trademark four-plane diamond formation. *Rich Kolasa*

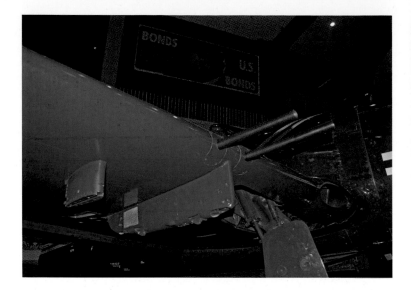

Under the starboard wing of the F8F-2P are a pylon for a bomb or drop tank, next to which is one of two smaller pylons for mounting a rocket. Fighter and night-fighter versions of the Bearcat featured these same pylons.

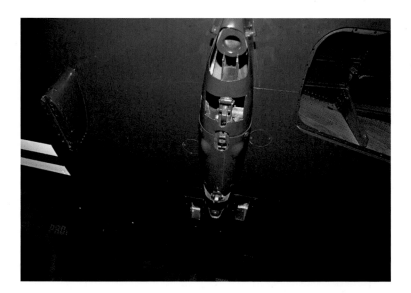

The bomb/drop-tank pylon and the inboard rocket pylon under the starboard wing of the F8F-2P are viewed facing aft. Aft of the larger pylon are two rectangular ports for ejecting spent 20 mm ammunition casings. The main gear wheel well is to the right.

The main landing-gear strut door (the starboard one is shown) covered much of the landing-gear bay when the landing gear was retracted. The two main landing-gear wheel doors, hinged at the inboard edges of the landing-gear bays, covered the remainder of the bay when the landing gear was retracted. This F8F-2P at the National Museum of Naval Aviation is marked to represent the aircraft of the Commander Air Group 19 and, accordingly, has "100" stenciled on the fuselage and landing-gear doors. The forward part of the wing bomb/drop-tank pylon is also visible in the background.

The same starboard main landing-gear unit seen at left is viewed here from the inboard side. To the front of the bottom of the oleo strut is the hydraulic brake. Above the wheel on the oleo strut, pointing forward, is the antitorque link, which kept the axle aligned at a right angle to the longitudinal centerline of the aircraft. The horizontal ring on the inboard side of the axle is a towing eye, which also facilitates mooring the aircraft. Further tie-down fittings were located on the main landing-gear trunnions and at the rear of the fuselage.

The starboard main landing gear of the F8F-2P at the National Museum of Naval Aviation is observed from the front. To the right of the tire is the front of the hydraulic brake and the towing/tie-down eye. To the left of the tire and landing-gear oleo strut is the landing-gear strut door. This is fastened to the oleo strut and fits tightly against the strut and the tire. The top of the oleo strut is fitted, via a pivoting mount, to the bottom of the main landing-gear trunnion. When the landing gear retracted, the trunnion swings outboard (*to the left in the photo*) while the oleo strut and wheel swing inward.

A 150-gallon drop tank is on the centerline mount under the fuselage of an F8F-2P. This tank carried fuel to supplement the 185-gallon pressurized main fuel tank below the cockpit. It was also possible to mount 100-gallon drop tanks on the wing pylons.

A bright-orange or red vapor vent and filler cap are visible atop the 150-gallon drop tank, seen here from the forward left side. The front adjustable sway brace, which held the tank tight in its mount, is visible.

One of a number of privately owned Bearcat survivors is this F8F-2, BuNo 122637, shown here with wings folded. This plane competed in a number of air-racing events, including several National Championship Air Races in the 1970s.

This look at the starboard side of F8F-2, BuNo 121748, reveals how the 150-gallon drop tank rests in its mount beneath the fuselage. The ground clearance of the rear of the drop tank is also visible. The sliding canopy was jettisonable in an in-flight emergency. To do this, the pilot pulled back on a red T-handle at the top of the canopy and then pushed the top front of the canopy up, allowing the airstream to pop off the canopy. *Stan Piet collection*

F8F-2, BuNo 121748 (D-224), rests on a hardstand. In actual US Navy service, this color scheme, with yellow and red stripes on the rudder trim tab and a red squadron marking on the top of the rudder and vertical stabilizer, was about as decorative as it got. *Stan Piet collection*

Although the US Navy Blue Angels flew Grumman F8F-1 Bearcats, this F8F-2, betrayed by its taller tail, has been restored in a Blue Angels paint scheme and markings. The current owner is John O'Connor, and the pilot this day was Freddie Cabanas. *Rich Kolasa*

The F8F-2 owned by John O'Connor in US Navy Blue Angels markings takes off, showing the main landing gear being retracted while also providing an excellent view of the fighter from the rear. A drop tank is on the centerline mount below the fuselage. *Rich Kolasa*

Notwithstanding the lack of 20 mm cannon barrels protruding from the wings, the two streamlined blisters on top of each wing, the tilted rear frame on the cockpit canopy, and the tall tail mark this as an F8F-2. In addition to the Blue Angels blue paint scheme, the markings on Blue Angels Bearcats were in a yellow color designated Gold. Each of the original planes had a number on the tail, 1 to 5. *Rich Kolasa*

This F8F-2 repainted in US Navy Blue Angels colors and markings is viewed from below. The original planes had "US Navy" in gold block letters under each wing. In July 1949, the Blue Angels traded in their F8F-1s for Grumman F9F-2 Panthers. On the port wing near the fuselage and immediately aft of the main landing-gear doors is the port dive-recovery flap. There is one under the starboard wing as well. *Rich Kolasa*

Grumman F8F-2P, BuNo 121710, at the National Museum of Naval Aviation, presents a sleek appearance in its glossy blue paint and Commander Air Group 19 markings. Noticeable here are the ribs, visible through the fabric skin of the starboard flap.

The instrument panel of the F8F-2P at the National Museum of Naval Aviation is characteristic of day-fighter and photoreconnaissance models of the Bearcat. It is compactly arranged, with cutouts on each lower side to provide room for the pilot's legs. At the top of the instrument panel is the Mk. 23 reflecting gunsight, with its tilted reflector plate above the body of the sight. Radar-equipped Bearcats substituted a radar scope for the instrument directly below the gunsight, the gyro horizon indicator. In front of the pilot's seat (*bottom*) is the control stick.

Below the instrument panel are the rudder pedals. Above the left console is the throttle quadrant, which contains the fuel mixture control (with the red knob marked "M"), the propeller pitch control (black knob with "P"), and throttle control (with silver grip).

More of the left console of an F8F-2P is shown. To the top right is the standby compass; below it is an air-vent nozzle. The wheel on the side of the console is the elevator trim tab control. The rectangular opening at the rear of the console is the map case.

In a view looking down into the right side of the cockpit, part of the pilot's seat, with the shoulder restraint and seat belt, is at the bottom of the photo. The lever with black grip next to the seat is the hydraulic hand pump. On the right console (*top of photo*) are radio controls.

In a view through the starboard side of the cockpit canopy of an F8F-2P, on the flat deck is a guide track for the sliding canopy. The rollover crash-protection arch can be seen through the canopy in its position behind the pilot's seat.

F8F-2, BuNo 121748 (D-224), and F8F-2, BuNo 122637 (F-225), fly in close formation. Too late to see combat in World War II and quickly rendered obsolete by jet fighters, the Bearcat nevertheless rendered useful service in the US Navy and US Marine Corps in the early years of the Cold War. In addition, Bearcats served in the air forces of several of the United States' allies in Southeast Asia. And, as one of the Blue Angels' first airplanes, the Bearcat demonstrated to the American populace the flying prowess of Navy aviators. *Rich Kolasa*

An F8F-1, as indicated by the taped-over .50-caliber machine gun ports on the wings, is spotted on the flight deck of USS *Valley Forge* (CV-45) during a visit of members of the American Ordnance Association, at Long Beach, California, on April 27, 1949. This plane was assigned to Fighter Squadron 111 (VF-111) "Sundowners," part of Carrier Air Group 11. The "V" tail code of CVG-11 is present on the Bearcat's left wing. By this date, Bearcat production was almost over, although the type would continue to fly in the service of the US Navy and other nations for several more years.